Squall Line on the Horizon
Tanka

Pris Campbell

Nixes Mate Books
Allston, Massachusetts

Copyright © 2017 Pris Campbell

Book design by d'Entremont

Cover photo by Michael McInnis

All rights reserved. This book or any portion thereof may not be reproduced or used in any manner whatsoever without the express written permission of the publisher except for the use of brief quotations in a book review or scholarly journal.

Some of these tanka appeared in the following journals, *Nixes Mate Review*, *A Hundred Gourds*, *cattails*, *Hedgerow*, *Frameless Sky*, and *Moonbathing*

ISBN 978-0-692-85080-0

Nixes Mate Books
POBox 1179
Allston, MA 02134
nixesmate.pub/books

For my husband Steve,
who understands that love doesn't limit itself.

Squall Line on the Horizon
Tanka

a witches moon
rests on my housetop tonight
I pluck
ghost figures from the air,
light one candle and wait

mortar shakes
the vietnamese forests
tour over
your ship steams into Pearl
lei around my neck quivering

bloom-plump bushes
glow under a lover's moon
rosebud
you sigh into my ear,
my petals opening wide

the sounds
of two dogs mating
you rouse me
to blue velvet kisses
on that bed junked by time

wars stench
permeates the air between us -
shouting
'you invade my space',
door slammed behind you

my lei
floats away with the tide
aloha
to where my soul dances
its dance of home found

another night lost
to the deceptive breeze
we make
the four legged monkey,
oblivious to its end

sleet coats
the old maple...
we once
shared everything but now,
so quickly, your eyes glaze

mist isolates
our old Boston brownstone
at arms length
after five long years,
beaten down I pack my bags

once, you and I
throughout the night
gardenias
scent the steamy air
reminding me of kisses past

breathing fire
you appear in my dream
sweat-soaked
I fight to escape the grasp
you still hold on my heart

last time...
I'm glad this particular last time
was you
whispering 'I always loved you'
on a purloined telephone

the pull
of oars against blue
some days
life's elusive rainbows
sit upstream taunting

en pointe
center stage left
wishes return
of swan wings lifting me
back to your waiting arms

wind-burst
through the honeysuckle
my feet
rush to meet you in places
you no longer are

the screech
of an unseen bird
heart fluttering
I wake to those things
that will or won't be again

empty sea shells
left at the high tide line
sometimes
I wonder which beach the me
I used to be wanders now

bells toll
beyond the knoll
the joy
held back since days with you
waits only for me to reclaim it

your heart
is finally open
how ironic
that a surgeon touches
what I never could

chill drives
away the lingering crows
your body
so shockingly shrunken,
my prince of lost dreams

cloaked by clouds
that morphine moon
your spirit
slip-slides each night
back to that old war

blackbird
already in flight
the worst part
is not being able to say
words you'll now never hear

nest scattered
by a late night storm
parts of me
seen by no-one but you,
lost now in your absence

mountaintop
imprinting the moon
your heart
remains connected to my heart
from somewhere outside the stars

you slide
through a slice in time
a soft touch
halts tears, shows me hope
in the afterglow of absence

helicopter
loud in the night
six months dead
and I still sometimes imagine
you're really back in Vietnam

along the pilings
a snail makes its way
I slowly move
through the dying dregs
of what was once vibrant

a hard wind
rises in the night...
pine cones
fly into the trembling pond
set sail for the moon

clearing the soil
for a new planting
mother's letter
stuck among old papers
asks my flight number home

leaves turn gold
at my old front yard
only in photos
do I still see lilies bend
in the breeze by the door

pageland,
always a safe haven
my heart
turns back to silver queen corn
and fried chicken sizzling

thorned roses
braided through my hair
the blush
on my cheeks deepens
with this first man after you

yellow daisies
left on my doorstep
love letters
I carefully decipher
petal by petal

fool on the hill
the beatles sang
dare I trust
letting him walk me
down that familiar path again

hothouse flowers
fill my parents' home
still uncertain,
my hand is sweaty
when he slips on the ring

the butterfly
flits from bloom to bloom
he tries to stay
faithful but never can
resist a new pretty face

his and her footprints
headed the other way
my new husband
abruptly becomes an etching
in the landscape of my life

seaweed
marks the tideline
I clear
my heart's debris in the wake
of his desertion

mother scissors him
from each wedding photo
timeless
I stand next to the black hole
that almost sucked my heart away

boulders
across my path
those times
I can't push through rough patches
the soft meadow grass soothes

the old oak
unexpectedly dies
a bare spot
where his wedding ring sat
looks suddenly pale

embers shift
in the fireplace grate
sudden warmth
from toes to fingertips
ignites old longings again

a seagull
shatters a clam on the rocks
exposing myself
to the sea's uncertainty
I head out

the sun drops
low on the horizon
I still blush
thinking of red-dress nights
when you wanted me

moonlight covers
the turtle's thick shell
wanting
but unable to make the stars
my protective canopy

pearl harbor
featured on a tv special
I slip back
to us, white beside white,
beneath that flashing sword arch

bees swarm
our night-blooming cactus
long gone
those times when men chased
after my swaying hips

the lap
of water against my bow
everywhere
the ghost moon swims with me
to places I search for you

winds rise
over the frothing sea
sails full
I fly with arms open
to greet what destiny brings

he said she said
in that game of gossip
I learn
endings are never
where the story began

squall line
on the far horizon
heart pounding
I double reef my sails
for whatever the night brings

a cat howls
outside my window
up all night
for different reasons
than when I was younger

dare I –
he asks for a dance
thirty-five years
now and counting
he still holds me close

fire burning
down to embers
settled
with my last solid love,
wilder days gone to time's sand

cinderella
pretty in her tiara
I've learned
fairytale lovers vanish
when pumpkins appear

surf pounds
against the distant beach
I long
to dance with dolphins again,
set my bed afloat, cast off

About the Author

The free verse poetry of Pris Campbell has appeared in numerous journals, such as *PoetsArtists. Rusty Truck, Bicycle Review, Boxcar Poetry Review*, and *Outlaw Poetry Network*. She has had three Pushcart nominations. Her haiku, tanka and haiga publications include *Frogpond, cattails, Acorn, Haigaonline, One Hundred Gourds*, and *Failed Haiku.* The Small Press has published six collections of her free verse poetry and Clemson University Press a seventh one, a collaboration. A former Clinical Psychologist, sailor and bicyclist until sidelined by ME/CFS in 1990, she makes her home in the Greater West Palm Beach, Florida.

Nixes Mate is a navigational hazard in Boston Harbor first used by colonists to graze their sheep. The island became infamous after the bodies of convicted pirates were gibbetted there to serve as warnings to mutinous sailors.

Nixes Mate Books features small-batch artisanal literature, created by writers that use all 26 letters of the alphabet and then some, honing their craft the time-honored way: one line at a time.

Other Nixes Mate titles:
ON BROAD SOUND | Rusty Barnes
KINKY KEEPS THE HOUSE CLEAN | Mari Deweese

Forthcoming titles from Nixes Mate Books:
HITCHHIKING BEATITUDES | Michael McInnis
LUBBOCK ELECTRIC | Anne Elezabeth Pluto
COMES TO THIS | Jeff Weddle
NIXES MATE REVIEW ANTHOLOGY 2016/17
STORIES | Lauren Leja

nixesmate.pub/books

www.ingramcontent.com/pod-product-compliance
Lightning Source LLC
Chambersburg PA
CBHW051957290426
44110CB00015B/2287